Rocky Mountain National Park

POCKET GUIDE

Stewart M. Greer

GUILFORD, CONNECTICUT
HELENA, MONTANA

AN IMPRINT OF THE GLOBE PEQUOT PRESS

FACT SHEET

History

Established: January 26, 1915

Visitors in 2006: 2,927,921

Physical Features

Acreage: 265,904.41 acres

Area: 416 square miles

Tallest peak: Longs Peak (14,259 feet)

Peaks over 10,000 feet: 113

Peaks over 12,000 feet: 72

Trail Ridge Road high point: 12,183 feet

Lakes: 147

Lakes with fish: approximately 50

Major rivers: Colorado, Cache la Poudre, Big Thompson, St. Vrain

Designated wilderness: 2,917 acres

Tundra: 87,700 acres

Species count: 65 mammals, 281 birds, 900 plants

Number of elk: More than 3,000 in summer

Annual precipitation: 14.79 inches on the east side (Estes Park); 20.36 inches on the west side (Grand Lake)

Facilities

Major road: Trail Ridge Road (48 miles long)

Trails: 355 miles

Campgrounds: 5, with 5 campsites

Backcountry campsites: 267

Picnic areas: 20

Permanent employees: 172

Seasonal employees: 20

Visitor centers: 4

Volunteers: 2,023

Volunteer hours: 97,401

Contents

Welcome:
Introduction to Rocky Mountain National Park

Rocky Mountain National Park. The name itself tells its story. This park offers simply the best of the Rocky Mountains, that long chain of mountains that stretches down western North America from Canada to New Mexico. This enormous and majestic parkland is many things: a haven of pristine ecosystems; a refuge for elk, bighorn sheep, mountain lion, and eagle; a land of quiet recreation—hiking, climbing, and nature study; an unpolluted watershed; and a place to grow and learn about the natural world, to catch a glimpse into nature's secret work.

As Colorado's largest national parkland, with 265,904 acres, Rocky Mountain National Park protects one of America's most beautiful and unspoiled mountain areas. This pristine swathe of high country

The Big Thompson River tumbles through Spruce Canyon just west of Moraine Park.

straddles the Continental Divide, the twisting backbone of North America that splits the Atlantic and Pacific Ocean watersheds. Designated an International Biosphere Reserve by the United Nations, the park boasts 113 named peaks above 10,000 feet, 72 topping 12,000 feet, and 19 over 13,000 feet. Longs Peak, its highest point, reaches 14,259 feet.

These high mountain peaks, snowcapped for much of the year, tower above broad glacier-carved valleys floored with meandering rivers and meadows and filled with roaming herds of elk, bighorn sheep, and mule deer. More than 150 lakes across the park reflect sky and cloud, and nearly 500 miles of streams and rivers thread through valleys and canyons. Rocky Mountain is a mother of rivers: Four great rivers—the Colorado, Cache la Poudre, Big Thompson, and St. Vrain—originate from its mountain snowpack. The park is also a land above the trees. One-third of the park lies in the treeless Alpine life zone, a cold, windswept land where summer visits for only two months a year.

In fact, the park offers remarkably diverse life zones, ecosystems, and animal habitats. Driving from Moraine Park to the top of Trail Ridge Road is like taking a telescoped journey from Colorado to the Arctic. As you drive upward on the twisted, switchbacked road, the air chills about 3 degrees every 1,000 feet, and precipitation increases. At lower elevations you'll see open stands of ponderosa pine on sunny hillsides, Douglas fir on shaded slopes, and broad open meadows. Climb higher and you'll discover stands of subalpine fir and blue

and Engelmann spruces and moist meadows carpeted with wildflowers, including the delicate columbine, Colorado's state flower. Head above the tree line into a world of extremes—where extreme winds, extreme cold, extremely long winters, and extremely short summers stunt trees into spare, twisted pygmy forests. This lofty yet fragile realm harbors perennial tundra plants, over one-quarter of which are found in the Arctic, that are superbly adapted to this extreme land above the trees.

Rocky Mountain is not just about stunning scenery; it's one of America's premier wildlife parks. Elk, bighorn sheep, and mule deer regularly graze in meadows and willow thickets near roadside viewing areas. In your travels you

Hallett Peak towers above lily-covered Nymph Lake in the calm before an afternoon thunderstorm.

may glimpse moose, coyotes, marmots, raptors, and songbirds. Time your visit to the fall rutting period and you'll see bull elk bugle their mating calls, vie for herd dominance, and gather harems of cows. It's a scene not soon forgotten.

You'll find countless ways to explore Rocky Mountain. Start with Trail Ridge Road, the highest continuously paved highway in the United States and a National Scenic Byway, a spectacular 48-mile scenic drive that climbs to 12,183 feet. Then step out of your car: More than 350 miles of trails traverse the park. For families or folks who don't want a strenuous walk, the park offers many easy and moderate hikes to fill an afternoon. Adventurers wear packs into the backcountry to campsites beside serene lakes or use their hands and feet to ascend vertical rock faces like the sheer Diamond on Longs Peak or the granite crags at Lumpy Ridge. The park offers convenient overlooks with scenic vistas, ranger-led interpretive programs and hikes, a Junior Ranger program for kids, camping in 587 sites in five campgrounds, and educational field seminars through the Rocky Mountain Nature Association. Rocky Mountain National Park awaits you—spin its magic into your adventure.

Navigate:
Getting to and around the park

Getting to the Park

Rocky Mountain National Park is easily accessed by major highways from Colorado's northern Front Range cities, including Denver, Boulder, Longmont, Loveland, Greeley, and Fort Collins. No air, rail, or bus service goes directly to the park. Estes Park Shuttle (970-586-5151) runs between Denver and Estes Park. Rental cars are available in Estes Park (limited) and all Front Range cities and at Denver International Airport.

Car: From Denver and points east, follow U.S. Highway 36 or Interstate 25 and U.S. Highway 34 to Estes Park. Denver is 65 miles (105 kilometers) away. Cheyenne, Wyoming, is 90 miles (145 kilometers) away. From Interstate 70 and the west and south, follow U.S. Highway 40 and US 34 to Grand Lake and the park's west entrance.

Plane: From Denver International Airport (800-AIR-2DEN; www.flydenver.com), the park is 67 miles (107.8 kilometers) to the northwest.

Train: Granby Train Station, serviced by Amtrak, is the nearest passenger terminal. There is no public transportation between the station and the park. Rental cars and taxi service are available.

Park Entrances

Rocky Mountain National Park is open twenty-four hours a day year-round. Visitors can enter and exit the park at any time through three main entrances: two in Estes Park on the east or one in Grand Lake on the west. These entrances are connected by Trail Ridge Road, which is open only in summer and fall. Most visitors enter the park from the east.

Beaver Meadows Entrance, west of Estes Park and just west of Beaver Meadows Visitor Center on US 36, leads to Moraine Park Museum, Moraine Park Campground, the Bear Lake area, and Trail Ridge Road.

Fall River Entrance, north of Beaver Meadows Entrance, enters the park on US 34 northwest of Estes Park. This entrance allows easy access to Old Fall River Road and Trail Ridge Road.

Grand Lake Entrance, the western terminus of Trail Ridge Road, is on US 3 north of Grand Lake.

Entrance Fees and Parking

There are several types of park entry passes. All are sold at park entrance stations:

Finding the Park

- Seven-day automobile pass for individuals or families: $20
- Seven-day pass for bicycles, motorcycles, mopeds, and pedestrians: $10 per individual; not to exceed $20 per vehicle
- Unlimited Rocky Mountain National Park entry pass: $35 annually
- National Parks and Federal Recreational Lands Pass: $80 annually

All vehicles must be driven only on roads or parked in designated areas. Do not park your vehicle or leave it unattended on park roads for more than twenty-four hours without prior permission from park headquarters. Hitchhiking is discouraged.

If you're staying overnight in the park, you must stay in a designated campground or camp in the backcountry

Tip: For updated park info and closures, visit the park's Web site at www.nps.gov/romo or call the park office at (970) 586-1206. For twenty-four-hour recorded information, call (970) 586-1333.

campsite with a valid permit. A fee is charged for all park campsites.

Getting around the Park

Only a few roads explore Rocky Mountain, leaving most of the park as wilderness reached only by foot trail. Trail Ridge Road (US 34), the park's main thoroughfare, runs 42 miles over lofty Trail Ridge and reaches elevations above 12,000 feet. The paved highway, closed by snow from late October to Memorial Day, rur

n Estes Park on the east to Grand
e on the west. Other park roads are
one-way, gravel Old Fall River Road,
ch climbs from Horseshoe Park to
ine Visitor Center; and paved 9-mile-
g Bear Lake Road. The southeast edge
he park, including Longs Peak and
d Basin, is accessed from Colorado
hway 7 south of Estes Park.

Two free shuttle routes will take you
ng the Bear Lake Road corridor and
Moraine Park during the very popular
mmer months. Since traffic conges-
n and limited parking at both Glacier
rge and Bear Lake Trailheads make
a major headache, especially on
sy weekends, leave your vehicle at
pacious Park & Ride parking lot and
e the shuttle buses to enjoy the scenic
ractions and loop hikes in these areas.
uttle buses run frequently from the

Park & Ride parking area opposite Glacier
Basin Campground to Bear Lake, as well
as from other bus stops including many
trailheads, Moraine Park Museum, and
Moraine Park Campground.

The Bear Lake shuttle runs every ten
to fifteen minutes, while the Moraine
Park shuttle runs every thirty minutes.

*Taking the shuttle is a smart way to get around
the park on busy summer days.*

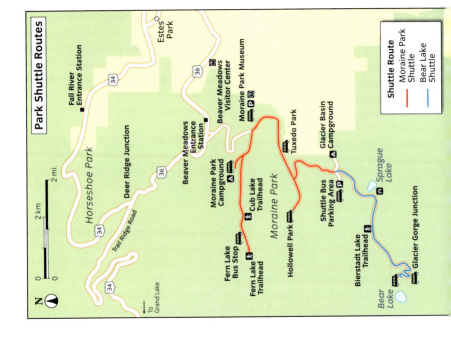

Park Shuttle Routes

Shuttle Route
Moraine Park Shuttle
Bear Lake Shuttle

N

2 km
2 mi.

Estes Park

Fall River Entrance Station

Horseshoe Park

Deer Ridge Junction

Trail Ridge Road

To Grand Lake

34
36

Beaver Meadows Entrance Station

Beaver Meadows Visitor Center

Moraine Park Museum

Tuxedo Park

Moraine Park Campground

Cub Lake Trailhead

Moraine Park

Hollowell Park

Glacier Basin Campground

Sprague Lake

Shuttle Bus Parking Area

Fern Lake Bus Stop

Fern Lake Trailhead

Bierstadt Lake Trailhead

Glacier Gorge Junction

Bear Lake

e first bus departs from the Park
ide stop at 7:00 a.m. and the last
s leaves at 7:00 p.m. The last bus
ves Bear Lake and Fern Lake Trail-
ads at 7:30 p.m. Call (970) 586-1206
updated shuttle schedules and
ormation.

sitor Centers

en you enter Rocky Mountain
tional Park, make one of the park's
r visitor centers your first stop. The
ters, staffed by park rangers and
unteers, orient you to the park,
er interpretative displays, dispense
uable information and permits, and
swer your important questions.

aver Meadows Visitor Center
'0-586-1206) is 2.5 miles west of Estes
·k on US 36. This center doubles
park headquarters and offers an

audiovisual program, a relief model of
the park, an excellent selection of books
and maps, and a short trail. Open daily
year-round 8:00 a.m. to 4:30 p.m., with
extended summer hours; closed only on
Christmas Day.

Fall River Visitor Center (970-586-1206)
is just outside the park boundary on US
34 before the Fall River entrance and 5
miles northwest of Estes Park. It features
animal exhibits (including full-size bronzes
of elk and other animals), a children's
Discovery Room, information desk, and
bookstore. Next door is the Rocky Mountain Gateway Store. Open daily in summer
9:00 a.m. to 5:00 p.m. and on winter
weekends 9:00 a.m. to 4:00 p.m.

Alpine Visitor Center (970-586-1206) is
25 miles west of Estes Park. This center
sits high atop Trail Ridge Road at 11,796
feet and explains life in the fragile tundra

Interpretive displays, such as this one by Sprague Lake, educate visitors about the park's history, natural history, and geology.

zone above tree line. After visiting the displays, step onto a wildlife observation platform that overlooks Fall River Gorge or hike the paved 0.25-mile Tundra Trail. Open daily in summer 9:00 a.m. to 5:00 p.m. and from September through mid-October 10:00 a.m. to 4:30 p.m.

Kawuneeche Visitor Center (970-62 3471) lies 1.3 miles north of Grand Lak on US 34. This western gateway to the park offers exhibits about the natural h tory, geology, wildlife, and human histo of the park's western sector. Especially popular is a 3-D topographical relief ma of Rocky. Open daily year-round 8:00 a.m. to 4:30 p.m., with extended hours summer.

Visitor Services

The park offers only basic visitor servic and amenities.

Emergencies and medical services

In case of emergency, dial 911 or call th park emergency line at (970) 586-1203 Emergency call boxes are located at W Basin Ranger Station, Longs Peak Rang Station, Lawn Lake Trailhead, Hidden V

Ranger Station, Cow Creek Trailhead, d Bear Lake Parking Lot.

Both Estes Park and Granby, on the st and west sides of the park respecely, offer twenty-four-hour emergency re.

- Estes Park Medical Center, P.O. Box 2740, 555 Prospect Avenue, Estes Park, CO 80517; (970) 586-2317; www.epmedcenter.com
- Granby Medical Center, 480 East Agate Avenue, Granby, CO 80446; (970) 887-2117

st and found. Make lost and found aims at the park Backcountry Office at 70) 586-1242.

stal services. Mailboxes are at Bea-r Meadows and Kawuneeche Visitor nters. Post offices are in Estes Park d Grand Lake.

> **Tip:** The Trail Ridge Store, with a snack bar and souvenirs, is next door to the Alpine Visitor Center.

Restrooms: At all four visitor centers, Moraine Park Museum, park camp-grounds, several picnic areas, Bear Lake, Sprague Lake, Lawn Lake Trailhead, Milner Pass, and Timber Lake Trailhead.

Telephones: Beaver Meadows, Fall River, and Kawuneeche Visitor Centers and at park campgrounds.

No gas stations, laundries, or public showers are in the park. Full visitor ser-vices are found outside the park in Estes Park to the east and Grand Lake to the west—services such as banks, ATMs, film processing and digital camera supplies, gas stations and mechanics, medical and dental services, churches, laundry facilities, public showers, restaurants, grocery stores, and accommodations including hotels, motels, and private campgrounds. Internet access is available in Estes Park and Granby.

Park Rules

Respect your park. Do not disturb or damage any natural feature, cultural resources, or park property. Removal of plants, rocks, fossils, or anything else is prohibited. Do not pick, collect, or damage any plants, including flowers. In addition, please heed these park regulations:

Bicycles. Cycling is allowed only on park roads and parking areas. No trail riding or backcountry bike travel is allowed.

Camping. Camp only at designated campgrounds and campsites.

Firearms. All weapons are prohibited, including air pistols and rifles, bows and arrows, crossbows, and slingshots. The use of fireworks and firecrackers is also banned.

Fires. Gathering firewood is prohibited. Bring your own wood or purchase it at campgrounds or nearby towns. Fires may be built in established fire pits with grates only. Put out fires properly.

Fishing. Angling requires a valid Colorado fishing license. Adults must use flies or artificial lures in all park waters. Children age twelve and under may use bait in open park waters, but not in catch-and-release sectors. Stop at a visitor center for information.

Pets. Pets are allowed in campgrounds, picnic areas, and along roads, provided they are on leashes not exceeding 6

et. They must be under control at all
nes and never left unattended, even in
hicles. Pets are not permitted on trails,
the backcountry, or in any park build-
g. Owners must clean up after their
t. Kennels are available in Estes Park.

hicles. Vehicles must stay on park
ads and in parking areas. Stopping or
rking is allowed only in designated
eas. All Colorado driving laws are in
rce, including child-restraint and seat-
lt laws. No open containers of alco-
lic beverages are allowed in vehicles
park roads.

ildlife. Feeding, touching, harassing,
hunting wildlife is prohibited. This
cludes stalking animals for photogra-
hy or using lights to spot wildlife.

Safety

Despite its sublime beauty Rocky Mountain National Park is also dangerous. The
park's extreme seasons and changeable
weather, coupled with elevation, can
quickly create problems for visitors.

Accidents and falls. Waterfalls, creeks,
and rivers are dangerous. Watch for slick
rocks along the banks, deceptively deep
and swift currents, and high water during
spring runoff. Climbing requires proper
training and equipment. Do not attempt
rock and snow climbs or scramble up
steep slopes that are beyond your ability
and experience. Serious accidents occur
on snow and ice fields. Keep off steep
snow slopes and cornices to avoid ava-
lanches or out-of-control falls.

Altitude. The park's high elevations,
particularly those sites easily reached

by Trail Ridge Road, can be dangerous to persons with heart conditions and respiratory problems. Many visitors, especially those arriving from sea-level sites, experience altitude sickness. Less oxygen in the park's rarified air means shortness of breath, headaches, fatigue, nausea, insomnia, and a rapid heartbeat. The best cure is to descend to a lower elevation. Consult your doctor before traveling into the high mountains. Allow your body to acclimate for a couple days to the higher elevations before attempting strenuous activities.

Insects. Ticks can attach themselves to your skin, possibly transmitting tick fever, Rocky Mountain spotted fever, or Lyme disease. Wood ticks are active from as early as February until August in wooded areas below 9,000 feet. Use insect repellent, wear long pants, and check yourself and others thoroughly every few hours. If a tick attaches, disinfect the area and gently remove the tick. See a doctor if you have any localized swelling or fever in the weeks following a bite. The park also has mosquitoes, which are usually found in lowland wet areas. Wear insect repellent.

Storms. Come prepared for bad weather. Bring long pants, good shoes (preferably water repellent), a raincoat, and warm clothes. A benign summer day can change in fifteen minutes to a raging thunderstorm with lightning and snow. In fact, thunderstorms regularly occur on summer afternoons, especially in July and August, and snow can fall every month of the year. Plan your high-altitude hikes and climbs for the morning so you're off the peaks before storms set in. When hiking, be ready to turn around

avoid getting caught outside. If you
[ar]e caught outside, avoid ridges, sum-
[mi]ts, and exposed lone objects like a tall
[tre]e. Also be aware that lessened visibil-
[ity] and slick rocks during storms can lead
[to] accidents and falls. Hypothermia, the
[lo]wering of the body's core temperature
[du]e to cold and wet, is one of the great-
[es]t dangers and can lead to death.

[W]ater. Do not drink water without
[bo]iling it or using a purification system.
[Gi]ardia, a microscopic organism found
[in] lakes and creeks, can cause severe
[ab]dominal cramps, bloating, and diar-
[rh]ea if you drink contaminated water. It's
[be]st to carry your own water.

[W]ildlife can cause safety problems.
[W]atch for animals crossing park roads,
[pa]rticularly at dawn and twilight. Do not
[ap]proach deer or elk, particularly during
[th]e fall rut. The park's black bears are

dangerous if provoked, especially if cubs
are present. Do not feed the bears or
other wildlife, and keep all food stored
in airtight containers and out of sight in
your vehicle.

The park is also mountain lion country,
but these beasts are rarely encountered.
For safety's sake, however, keep children
with you while hiking. If you do meet a
lion, stop and walk backward slowly with
your arms raised to appear larger.

Weather

Weather conditions and temperatures
vary dramatically. Higher elevations are
cooler and wetter, while lower elevations are warmer and drier. Summer
is the best time to visit the park, with
daily highs in the 70s and 80s and lows
in the 40s. Thunderstorms often occur
during July and August, the wettest

Longs Peak and Mount Meeker dominate the southwest skyline from Lily Lake.

onths. Autumn days are cool and crisp. aily highs climb into the 60s and 70s, th occasional storms and even snow. inters are cold and snowy. Temperatures swing from the 50s to below zero egrees. The lower elevation areas can e mild even in January, the coldest onth. Spring is changeable with snow, ind, and warmth. Daily highs climb to e 50s and 60s. Snow can fall into June.

The wise traveler anticipates all onditions in this land of weather xtremes. Pack a raincoat and a warm cket for chilly nights and wind. Add a arm cap and gloves in spring and fall. unscreen, lip balm, and a hat protect gainst sunburn. Winter requires layers f warm clothes that can be easily put on r peeled off.

Important Park Contact Numbers

General park information: (970) 586-1206

Emergencies: 911 or (970) 586-1203

Backcountry Office: (970) 586-1242

Camping reservations: Glacier Basin, Moraine Park: (877) 444-6777

Estes Park Chamber of Commerce: (800) 378-3708

Estes Park Convention & Visitors Bureau: (800) 443-7837

Grand Lake Chamber of Commerce: (800) 531-1019

Lost and found: (970) 586-1242

Recorded information and road and weather conditions: (970) 586-1333

Rocky Mountain Nature Association: (800) 816-7662

History:
Key things about the park

Come to Rocky Mountain National Park with open eyes and heart and explore its rich geological and cultural history.

Geological History

Rocky Mountain National Park first and foremost offers a geology lesson, a tale of past history spread over billions of years. Few places boast the variety and age of the rock exposed here, ranging from metamorphic rocks almost two billion years old to deposits left by glaciers a scant 20,000 years ago. Here you see evidence of the earth's constant evolution—the raising and tearing down of mountain ranges and the coming and going of different life forms.

◀ *The Mushroom Rocks, composed of some of the park's oldest rocks, rise above Tundra Communities Trail high on Trail Ridge Road.*

The story begins more than 1.75 billion years ago during a geologic age called the Precambrian era. During this long span, the earth's crust solidified and granites formed ancient continents, which were then blanketed with eroded sediments. These in turn were heaved, twisted, and subjected to intense pressure and heat that formed metamorphic rocks—that is, rocks changed into new rocks like schist and gneiss.

In time new mountains rose and wore away, and oceans inundated the land then retreated. Few rock records exist for this 500-million-year period known as the Paleozoic and Mesozoic eras. We do know that a great range, the Ancestral Rockies, rose about 300 million years ago before being flattened. Then great fields of sand dunes crept across the land before the ocean again flooded it.

Some sixty-seven million years ago at the end of the Mesozoic era (the time of the dinosaurs), today's Rocky Mountains began a slow, sporadic uplift interrupted by long periods of erosion. The last uplift began seven million years ago. Extensive volcanism twenty-three million years ago was another factor in the formation of today's landscape in the western part of the park, including the Never Summer Range. During this time erosion attacked the rising mountains, carving valleys and shaping mountains.

Glaciation put the finishing touches on Rocky Mountain's topography approximately 1.6 million years ago, after the earth's climate dramatically cooled. During at least four major periods of glaciation, immense glaciers over 1,500 feet thick filled the mountain valleys, scraping their stony flanks into steep

ater, cloud reflections, and matted grasses surround a glacier-deposited boulder on the southern
ge of Sprague Lake.

cliffs and chiseling cirques, ridges, and peaks. The last two glacial periods—the Bull Lake and Pinedale glaciations—began 300,000 years and 30,000 years ago respectively, with a warm period in between. About 15,000 years ago a warming climate melted the glaciers. Today only a few miniglaciers (none remnants of the great valley glaciers) remain in shady cirques like that below Longs Peak's vertical east face. As you drive about the park, imagine the recent past when cold rivers of ice engulfed the green forested valleys, leaving only barren peaks projecting above a white, barren landscape of perpetual winter.

Human History

Native Americans roamed the Rocky Mountain region for the past 12,000 years. They visited on a seasonal basis, hunting wild game and gathering edible plants. After the arrival of Europeans in the New World, the Ute and Arapahoe tribes lived here, mostly in summer and fall, with the Arapahoes migrating in from Minnesota about 1790. At least thirty-six place-names in the park derive from Arapahoe names, including Lumpy Ridge, from *That-aa-ai-atah* or "Mountain with Little Lumps." They called Longs Peak and Mount Meeker *neniisotoyou'u*, meaning "there are two mountains."

The first Anglo visitors to the park were French fur trappers who dubbed Longs Peak and Mount Meeker *les Deux Oreilles,* or "the Two Ears." The first American reference to the peak was by Edwin James, a botanist on Maj. Stephen Long's expedition from Pittsburgh to the Rocky Mountains in 1820. James noted in his diary that the mountains presented a

...mpy Ridge is studded with soaring granite outcrops.

"grand outline, imprinted in bold indentations upon the luminous margin of the sky." Long, for whom the landmark peak is named, only saw the park's mountains from the prairie to the east. Rufus Sage, who roamed the Rockies for three years, spent a month in the area in 1843. He later recounted his adventures in *Scenes in the Rocky Mountains*, published in 1846.

The first recorded ascent of Longs Peak came on August 23, 1868, when one-armed Civil War veteran Maj. John Wesley Powell led a party of seven climbers to the flat summit. L. W. Keplinger later recounted that on the summit Powell took off his hat and gave a speech: "He said ... that we had now accomplished an undertaking ... which had hitherto been deemed impossible ... and predicted that what we had that day accomplished was but the augury of yet greater achievements."

The area's first settler was Kentuckian Joel Estes, who homesteaded here 1860. After six hard winters, he swapped the place for a yoke of oxen. Griff Evans took over the Estes place and added guest cabins. Settlers and other visitors arrived in droves late in the nineteenth century. Miners seeking gold in the north-west sector of the park founded Lulu C in the 1880s, and hunters decimated the area's big game. Tourists, hearing of the area's scenic beauty, also visited.

The National Park Idea

By the turn of the twentieth century, local environmentalists clamored for the area's preservation to save it from logging, hunting, mining, and development. Naturalist, climber, and writer Enos M who settled below Longs Peak in 1884 proposed that an area from Wyoming

Mount Evans become a national park. Local civic leaders—including O. Stanley, inventor of the Stanley Steamer and owner of the luxurious Stanley Hotel—took up the idea. After various compromises with mining and timber interests, today's Rocky Mountain National Park was established on January 26, 1915, by President Woodrow Wilson.

Sprague Lake reflects afternoon clouds and the shimmering Continental Divide.

Flora and Fauna:
All things great and small

The park's geography and elevation range determine its climate and precipitation, which in turn shape the lives of 900 species of plants, 281 types of birds, and 65 species of mammals. Lower elevations are warmer and drier, while higher elevations are cooler and wetter. Precipitation varies widely, with 14 inches of annual rainfall on the east side of the park, 20 inches on the west, and as much as 40 inches in the high mountains. Plants and animals have evolved to adapt to these conditions.

A Living Laboratory of Life Zones

Rocky Mountain National Park is a living laboratory that embraces three of Colorado's five life zones. Life zones are horizontal bands of

Columbines thrive in a subalpine meadow along Old Fall River Road.

vegetation that result from the adaptation and response of plants to precipitation, temperature, and weather at different elevations.

Montane life zone, occurring up to 9,000 feet, is characterized by sunny woodlands of ponderosa pine on south-facing slopes, Douglas fir on shaded north-facing slopes, groves of quaking aspen, and open meadowlands blanketed with grass and wildflowers. The meadows, along with creeks and wetlands filled with dense willow thickets, offer excellent animal habitats. Elk, bighorn sheep, and mule deer frequently graze the grassy meadows or browse along forest edges. Look for aspen trees scarred by browsing elk in search of sweet inner bark, beaver swimming in reflective ponds, and black tassel-eared Abert squirrels chattering in pines.

Subalpine life zone, lying between 9,000 and 11,400 feet, resembles the boreal forests of northern Canada. Long, cold winters with deep snow; short summers; and 30-plus inches of annual precipitation allow only hardy trees and plants to flourish. Dark forest of Englemann spruce and subalpine fir cover steep mountainsides, interrupted by stands of lodgepole pine and aspen. Twisted by wind, limber pine thrive on exposed ridges. Meadows, verdant in summer with grass, sedge, columbine, and shooting star, fill moist valleys. Animals living here include elk, mule deer, black bear, beaver, martens, and marmots. Common birds are Clark's nutcrackers, Stellar's jays, ruby-crowned kinglets, pine grosbeaks, and hermit thrushes.

The tree line, the transition zone between the Subalpine and Alpine life

Hungry elk scarred this aspen grove in Moraine Park by nibbling the bark in winter when deep snow buried grass and shrubs.

zones, is the upper limit for tree growth. Above tree line—roughly 11,400 feet in the park—the weather is simply too harsh for trees. Enos Mills called it "the line of battle between the woods and the weather." The strange krummholz (German for "crooked wood") woodland occurs at tree line, where wind-blasted trees form miniature forests. Tree growth is slow in the low temperatures, harsh winds, and short growing season. A 200-year-old tree might be only 4 inches in diameter and 4 feet tall. Look for krummholz forest on Trail Ridge Road as it climbs from Rainbow Curve to Ute Trail Overlook.

Alpine life zone, the fragile land above the trees, is Rocky Mountain's most unusual ecosystem with one-third of the park—more than 100 square miles—above tree line. During summer's six- to eight-week growing season, the tundra

Extreme Weather

As you rise in elevation, the air temperature cools about 3 degrees Fahrenheit every 1,000 feet in height. Park wind speeds reach as high as the 201-mile-per-hour gust recorded atop Longs Peak.

meadows are a colorful mass of wildflowers. Some 250 plant species grow above tree line in the Rockies. The flora hugs the ground in dense mats to mitigate the severe mountain climate. Alpine plants must adapt to harsh conditions to survive, including high winds, dry air, low soil moisture, and fierce sunlight. Most plants are perennial, because one summer is simply too short to complete their life cycles. Many are long lived,

Alpine avens on Chapin Pass nestle in a protective rocky crevice.

like alpine phlox, which lives as long as 150 years; some have taproots as long as 6 feet to gather moisture and anchor the plant against the wind. Other alpine plants include lichens and mosses. Alpine animals include pika, marmot, and white-tailed ptarmigan, and elk summer in the high country.

Wildlife

Watching wildlife is a favorite park activity. Most people come to glimpse the big critters, including elk, bighorn sheep, mule deer, and moose. In all almost 65 species of mammals, 281 species of birds, 11 fish, 6 amphibians, and 1 reptile inhabit the park.

Elk, or wapiti, abound in the park. In summer more than 3,000 of these majestic mammals roam from lower elevation meadows to the high country. During f the elk migrate down from the mounta for the annual rut or breeding season. Bull elk bugle, intimidate, and fight eac other for rights to harems of females. The bugle, eerily heard echoing across the valleys, is a strange and unforgettable call. In summer the elk roam the high country. Look for them feeding in meadows below Trail Ridge Road. Lowe elevation sightings are best in Septemb and October in open clearings at Kawu eeche Valley, Horseshoe Park, Moraine Park, and Upper Beaver Meadows.

Bighorn sheep, the park's symbol anc the Colorado state mammal, are a rugged, muscular mammal. Their hoofs, sc in the center and hard on the edges, ar ideal for scrambling across rock on stee mountain slopes. The park's herd range from 300 to 500 animals. At one time th

herd was decimated by domestic sheep and their diseases; by the 1950s bighorns numbered about 150. Conservation efforts, including controlling human access to lambing areas, increased the herd to present levels. Look for bighorns at roadside viewing areas at Sheep Lakes and Horseshoe Park, where they visit a natural mineral lick.

Moose, a nonnative species in Colorado, live on the west side of the park in Kawuneeche Valley. A relative of deer, moose can stand as tall as 7 feet and weigh almost a ton. They're ornery and unpredictable, especially in the fall mating season. Look for moose browsing in marshy willow thickets along the Colorado River, in beaver ponds north of

Elk, often seen grazing alongside Trail Ridge Road, are the park's best-known and best-loved animal.

Wildlife Watching Tips

- Best places to see wildlife: Trail Ridge Road (marmot, pika), Horseshoe Park (elk, bighorn sheep), Moraine Park (deer, elk), Coyote Valley Nature Trail (moose, deer, elk).
- If you stop your car to watch animals, pull off the road. Don't block traffic. Your car makes a perfect blind, so talk only when necessary and turn off the engine.
- Drive slowly on park roads and watch for wildlife crossing them. Deer and elk travel in groups. Watch for animals on roads at twilight.
- Always watch from a distance—your presence alters their behavior and stresses the animals. Use binoculars or a telephoto lens instead of stalking animals for close-up views and photos.
- Large mammals—elk, deer, moose, bighorn sheep, bear, and mountain lion—are dangerous. Don't get too close.
- Use of spotlights and wildlife calls are illegal.
- Don't feed panhandling animals like squirrels and deer. They become habituated to humans, can be run over by cars, and often become aggressive.

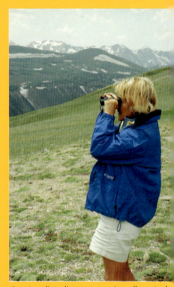

A naturalist glimpses grazing elk on Iceber Pass near Trail Ridge Road.

mber Creek Campground, and along
yote Valley and Onahu trails.

kas, a rabbit relative, are small, brown
ammals with large round ears. Pikas
e superbly adapted to life above tree
e. Living in groups in rock piles, pikas
end most of the warm months gather-
g grass, which they dry and then store
th cut alpine avens (which prevent rot
d mildew) in underground haystacks
r winter dinners. They use a distinctive
rill cry to warn others of predators.
kas are usually seen along Trail Ridge
ad. Stop at Rock Cut and hike up
ndra Communities Trail to spot these
ite critters.

Yellow-bellied marmots, a large
ground squirrel and relative of eastern
groundhogs, are stocky mammals with
coarse brown fur and a yellow belly.
They graze and forage in summer to
build up fat stores for the long winter
when they hibernate. The more fat, the
better chance a marmot has to survive
hibernation, when its body temperature
drops to 40 degrees and the animal loses
half its body fat. Marmots live in alpine
meadows as well as in lower elevations.
Look for them along Trail Ridge Road and
Old Fall River Road.

FLORA AND FAUNA

Horizons:
Natural and historic sites

Rocky Mountain National Park begins and ends with its geography—spiked mountains scraping against cloud bellies; hanging cirques and U-shaped valleys excavated by ancient glaciers; forests and meadows replete with wildflowers and wild animals. This place of natural wonders and hidden history humbles your civilized mind. The constant presence of landscape is always a reminder of the wild, that out there is a land of sky and granite, wind and snow.

Natural Wonders

Mountains and rivers are the heart and soul of Rocky Mountain National Park. They define its essence and they create its magic.

◄ *Jutting cliffs at Rock Cut on Trail Ridge Road frame Longs Peak, Rocky Mountain National Park's highest mountain.*

Longs Peak, Rocky Mountain's most distinctive feature, dominates Colorado's northern Front Range like no other peak. Longs, with its conspicuous flat summit, rises abruptly above lower mountains and is easily seen from 100 miles away. It's Colorado's fifteenth-highest peak at 14,259 feet high.

Mummy Range, resembling a reclining mummy from a distance, is a northeast-trending range in northern Rocky Mountain National Park. Prominent peaks in the range are 13,514-foot Ypsilon Mountain, with its distinctive Y-shaped couloir; 13,425-foot Mummy Mountain; and Hagues Peak, the 13,560-foot range high point. The peaks are easily accessed from the Ypsilon Lake and Lawn Lake trails.

Never Summer Mountains, topped by 12,940-foot Mount Richthofen, is

Cloud shadows trail across Longs Peak's abrupt east face, including the distinctive Diamond, a favorite rock-climbing venue.

0-mile-long range that forms the northwest boundary of Rocky Mountain National Park. The north-to-south-trending range is relatively young compared Rocky's other mountains, formed out 25 million years ago during a period of volcanism. Glaciation, ending 7,000 years ago, did the final sculpting. The range's poetic name comes from the Arapaho name *Ni-chebe-chii,* which translates to "Never No Summer." Trail Ridge Road offers great views of the range to the northwest.

Rivers. If one place in Colorado could be called the Mother of Rivers, this would be it. Four rivers—the Colorado, Cache la Poudre, Big Thompson, and St. Vrain—arise from snow on the park's crooked spine. The Colorado is the sixth longest of the 135 rivers in the United States, drains 242,000 square miles in seven states, and flows 1,440 miles from its humble origin atop the park's 10,758-foot Milner Pass to its mouth in the Gulf of California. The Cache la Poudre River, named for a hidden powder cache near today's Fort Collins, begins on the east side of Milner Pass. The Big Thompson River empties Trail Ridge and the Continental Divide, runs through Estes Park, and dashes down a sharp canyon to the plains. The St. Vrain River, also running east to the plains, begins with melting snow along the Divide above Wild Basin in the park's southern reaches.

Points of Interest

Alluvial Fan, on the Old Fall River Road 3 miles from the Fall River Entrance Station on the north side of Horseshoe Park, demonstrates the explosive forces of nature. On July 15, 1982, when a

Climbing Longs Peak

The park's first climbers were ancient hunters who crossed high mountain passes and undoubtedly scrambled to summits on vision quests. In 1914 Gun Griswold told how his father, Old Man Gun, a great warrior and hunter, made an eagle trap atop Longs Peak. Here he hid below a bison hide with a coyote pelt for bait. When an eagle landed, he grabbed its feet and bound them with cord.

Today Longs Peak is one of Colorado's most popular fourteeners, that elite group of fifty-four skyscraping peaks above 14,000 feet. Every year as many as 10,000 hikers and climbers reach the summit. Longs boasts more than a hundred routes on its rocky flanks, but most are technical rock climbs that require specialized gear and ropes as well as climbing skills and techniques. For the serious hiker, however, the excellent Keyhole Route, the only nontechnical climbing route, leads to the summit.

The Keyhole Route climbs 7.4 miles to the flat summit and gains 4,859 feet. The route is usually free from ice and snow from mid-July until mid-September. Objective dangers include thunderstorms, lightning, snow and sleet, slick rock and snowfields, falling rocks, and the sheer masses of people on the trail. The route can be very dangerous in bad weather, especially for inexperienced and ill-prepared hikers. A good summer weekend sees a hundred-plus people at a time on the summit. Begin early, plan to be off the summit before noon, and bring raincoats, warm clothes, and food.

The route begins at Longs Peak ...ilhead on the east side of the moun-...n; it corkscrews around the peak to ...sh up the south side. The first 5.9 miles ...low good trail to the Boulder Field at ...750 feet, then scrambles through the ...yhole. After scrambling 0.3 mile, the ...ite ascends the Trough, a rocky gully to ...e west ridge. Above it crosses onto the ...uth flank and traverses a ledge system ...led the Narrows. Finish up the slabby ...mestretch to the summit. Consult one ...the excellent comprehensive hiking ...des for a complete route description ...if you're inexperienced, hire a guide to ...ep you safe and lead you to the summit.

The distinctive flat summit of Longs Peak is reached by a difficult 7.4-mile trail.

The Roaring River cascades down bedrock exposed by the 1982 flood at Alluvial Fan.

all earthen dam failed, floodwater, ge boulders, and toppled trees ged down Roaring River and entered rseshoe Park. The resulting forty--acre alluvial fan contained piles of ky debris up to 44 feet deep. You can lore the alluvial fan by hiking a short erpretative trail across the debris field the base of a graceful cascade. For a od overall view of the fan, stop at Rain-w Curve overlook on Trail Ridge Road.

lzwarth Trout Lodge Historic Site.

1916 John Holzwarth Sr., a Denver bar-ep, homesteaded at this site perched ng the Colorado River in Kawuneeche ley; when Fall River Road was com--ted in 1920, he opened the lodge to velers. After ten years he switched to ude ranch operation, which ran until 72. Now you can visit the site as it was 1920 when guests paid $11 a week for

a room and two meals a day. Volunteers give guided tours. Check at a visitor center for tour times and site hours. The lodge is reached by a 0.5-mile trail on Trail Ridge Road, 8 miles north of the Grand Lake entrance station.

Lulu City. Rocky Mountain National Park was not exempt from Colorado's gold fever of the 1870s and 1880s. In 1880 Benjamin Burnett and William Baker platted a mining camp that they named Lulu City. By the following summer the town boasted 500 residents, two sawmills, a general store, a barbershop, a clothing store, an assay office, a hotel, a restaurant, a couple of stagecoach lines, a two-cabin red-light district, and forty homes. But it was all for naught, and by late 1883 the town was officially pronounced dead. Lulu City is now a ghost town of cabin ruins, rusted mining

Dudes relaxed on the front porch of the Mama Cabin while awaiting one of Mama Holzwarth's home-cooked meals.

equipment, tailings piles, and wagon ruts in wildflower-strewn meadows. The townsite is reached by 3.7-mile Lulu City Trail. (See the "Hiking" section in the G Going chapter.)

Moraine Park Museum, 2.5 miles southwest of Beaver Meadows Visitor Center on Bear Lake Road, is located in a historic 1923 log building. Designed by the Denver Museum of Nature and Science, the museum's displays examine Rocky's geology, natural history, plants, and animals. Kids enjoy moving faults and glaciers on scale models that illustrate these earth processes from the formation of Precambrian metamorphic rock to the last glaciation 15,000 years ago. In summer ranger-led hikes explore the surrounding area. Free admission. Open daily 9:00 a.m. to 5:00 p.m. in summer only.

Get Going:
Activities in the park

Rocky Mountain National Park is a place for doing, a place to get out of your car and onto the land. Spend the night outside under the stars. Hike a trail along a rushing stream. Inch your way up a granite cliff with air under your soles. Cast a homemade fly onto a lake that reflects blue sky. Make life an adventure.

Hiking

With 350-plus miles of trails, Rocky offers you a choice of many hikes, from easy strolls to challenging adventures. The park's foot-paths whisk you away from roads and parking lots into wild and scenic landscapes, past alpine lakes ringed with wind-swept grass, and into lofty valleys below shining mountains. The following are a few of Rocky's best hikes. For more hikes and maps, ask a ranger at a visitor for suggestions.

Alberta Falls Trail

Length: 0.6 mile (1.2 miles out and back).
Difficulty: Easy; 160-foot elevation gain.
Start: Glacier Gorge Trailhead.
This scenic stroll, climbing 160 feet, threads along tumbling Glacier Creek to Alberta Falls, one of the park's best waterfalls. From the falls, retrace your steps or hike another 1.9 miles to lovely Mills Lake.

Bear Lake Nature Trail

Length: 0.6-mile loop.
Difficulty: Easy.
Start: Bear Lake Trailhead.
Take this loop around scenic Bear Lake for spectacular views of Hallett Peak and

> He who feels the spell of the wild, the rhythmic melody of falling water, the echoes among the crags, the bird songs, the wind in the pines . . . is in tune with the universe.
>
> —ENOS MILL

Longs Peak. Most of the path is wheelchair accessible. Come early in the day for privacy.

Chasm Lake Trail

Length: 4.2 miles (8.4 miles out and bac
Difficulty: Difficult; 2,390-foot elevation gain.
Start: Longs Peak Trailhead.
One of the park's best hikes! Climb 2,3
feet to Chasm Lake, a spectacular alpir

lake nestled in a cirque below Longs Peak's great east face. Look for waterfalls, wildlife, and breathtaking views.

Cub Lake Trail

Length: 2.3 miles (4.6 miles out and back).
Difficulty: Moderate; 540-foot elevation gain.
Start: Cub Lake Trailhead on Cub Lake Road.
This excellent hike crosses the marshy west end of Moraine Park before climbing through a fir and pine woodland to yellow lily-covered Cub Lake.

Rugged Hallett Peak dominates the view from Bear Lake.

Emerald Lake Trail

Length: 1.8 miles (3.6 miles out and back).
Difficulty: Moderate; 605-foot elevation gain.
Start: Bear Lake Trailhead.
Hike up a glacial valley and pass Bear Lake, Nymph Lake, and Dream Lake, then end the hike at gleaming Emerald Lake below Hallett Peak's sheer east face. Spot wildlife, especially marmots, along the way.

Gem Lake Trail

Length: 2.0 miles (4.0 miles out and back).
Difficulty: Moderate; 1,090-foot elevation gain.
Start: Lumpy Ridge Trailhead.
This delightful hike through a ponderosa pine forest passes granite outcrops like Paul Bunyan's boot and ends at pretty Gem Lake tucked into a rock-walled valley. A good hike for kids. Usually warmer than other trails, making it a good bet for winter hiking.

Lulu City Trail

Length: 3.7 miles (7.4 miles out and back).
Difficulty: Moderate; 350-foot elevation gain.
Start: Colorado River Trailhead 9.5 miles north of Grand Lake entrance.
This fun and easy trail meanders through meadows and woodlands on the east side of the Colorado River, passes an old mine and cabin ruins, and then follows an old stage route to Lulu City, an 1880s ghost town.

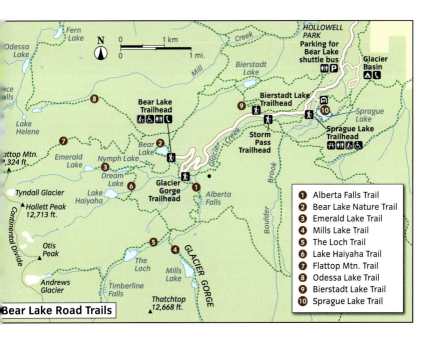

Bear Lake Road Trails

1. Alberta Falls Trail
2. Bear Lake Nature Trail
3. Emerald Lake Trail
4. Mills Lake Trail
5. The Loch Trail
6. Lake Haiyaha Trail
7. Flattop Mtn. Trail
8. Odessa Trail
9. Bierstadt Lake Trail
10. Sprague Lake Trail

Fern Lake

Odessa Lake

Mill Creek

HOLLOWELL PARK

Parking for Bear Lake shuttle bus

Glacier Basin

Bierstadt Lake

Bierstadt Lake Trailhead

Bear Lake Trailhead

Mill Creek

Glacier Creek

Sprague Lake

Sprague Lake Trailhead

Lake Helene

Bear Lake

Storm Pass Trailhead

Boulder Brook

Flattop Mtn. 12,324 ft.

Emerald Lake

Nymph Lake

Dream Lake

Glacier Gorge Trailhead

Alberta Falls

Lake Haiyaha

Tyndall Glacier

Hallett Peak 12,713 ft.

Continental Divide

Otis Peak

The Loch

Mills Lake

GLACIER GORGE

Andrews Glacier

Timberline Falls

Thatchtop 12,668 ft.

N

0   1 km

0   1 mi.

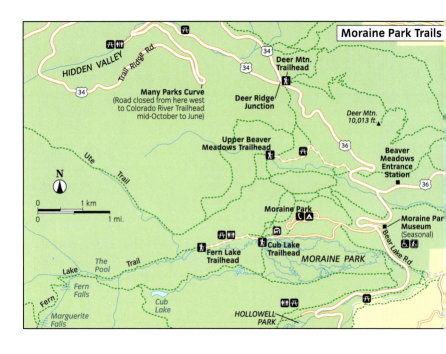

Moraine Park Trails

HIDDEN VALLEY

Trail Ridge Rd.

34

34

34

Many Parks Curve
(Road closed from here west
to Colorado River Trailhead
mid-October to June)

**Deer Mtn.
Trailhead**

**Deer Ridge
Junction**

*Deer Mtn.
10,013 ft.*

36

**Beaver
Meadows
Entrance
Station**

36

**Upper Beaver
Meadows Trailhead**

Ute Trail

N

0   1 km

0   1 mi.

Moraine Park

**Moraine Par
Museum**
(Seasonal)

**Fern Lake
Trailhead**

**Cub Lake
Trailhead**

MORAINE PARK

Bear Lake Rd.

The Pool

Trail

Lake

Fern

*Fern
Falls*

*Cub
Lake*

*Marguerite
Falls*

*HOLLOWELL
PARK*

ackpacking

ne of Rocky Mountain's finest outdoor
ventures is backpacking—sleeping
der a night sky studded with stars,
eading trails through flower-strewn
eadows, and renewing your soul in
e wilderness. Most of the park is wild
d untraveled, except by those willing
put one foot in front of the other. The
ther you get from the road, the more
litude you'll find.

It's easy to combine several of the
rk's shorter trails into a longer multi-
ay loop. Consider combining trails in
e Bear Lake, Loch, and Glacier Gorge
ea; doing a two-day backpack up
ongs Peak; or exploring Wild Basin in
e southern part of the park. Additional
cellent campsites, ideal for those who
e to fish, are found on the park's west
de.

Consult with rangers in the Backcountry Office, located near Beaver
Meadows Visitor Center, about your
proposed trek: a backcountry use permit
is required for all users. Reservations by
mail can be made through the office after
March 1 for the calendar year; write to
Backcountry/Wilderness Permits, Rocky
Mountain National Park, 1000 Highway
36, Estes Park, CO 80517. Or reserve
by phone at (970) 586-1242 between
March 1 and May 15 or after October
1. You can pick up a permit in person at
either the Beaver Meadows office or at
Kawuneeche Visitor Center. An online
Backcountry Camping Guide can be
downloaded from the park's Web site.
For more information visit www.nps.gov/
romo/planyourvisit/backcountry.htm.

Remember to practice no-impact,
leave-no-trace camping techniques:

Leave the park's fragile landscape just like you found it.

Bicycling

Rocky Mountain offers great road biking, but be prepared for the lung-busting altitude and long, strenuous climbs on grades up to 7 percent. Bicycling is permitted only on roads. No off-road or mountain biking is allowed on any trails.

A good bike ride is the 8-mile climb from Moraine Park to Bear Lake. If you bring a mountain bike, try the gravel 9.4-mile Old Fall River Road. Trail Ridge Road, climbing almost 4,000 feet in 20 miles, is one of America's most spectacular rides. Get an early start to avoid traffic and afternoon thunderstorms. Remember that Old Fall River Road is a one-way, up-only road.

Rock Climbing and Mountaineering

You'll experience some of the best alpine climbing in the United States on Rocky Mountain National Park's glaciated peaks. This vertical sanctuary hosts many classic routes on its renowned cliffs, including the Diamond on Longs Peak; Spearhead; Chiefshead; Petit Grepon; Hallett Peak; and Notchtop. These high cliffs have long tantalized and attracted climbers with their sublime rock and purity of ascent.

In the lower elevations is Lumpy Ridge, one of Colorado's best cragging areas. The ridge, studded with granite crags, stretches across Estes Park's northern skyline. The Arapaho Indians first named the ridge *That-aa-ai-atah,* or "Mountain with Little Lumps." Later set-

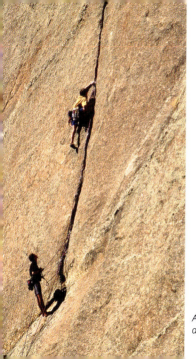

tlers simplified the name to Lumpy Ridge. The scattered crags that decorate Lumpy Ridge—including the Twin Owls, the Book, the Pear, and Sundance Buttress— yield excellent rock climbs.

Besides high-altitude technical climbing, which requires climbing gear and rock- and ice-climbing experience, the park offers mountaineering routes up steep snow chutes or scrambles up rocky faces. One of the best, of course, is the challenging ascent of Longs Peak. (See the "Climbing Longs Peak" sidebar for details.)

Technical climbing doesn't require permits, but climbers who plan to bivouac below their intended route need a backcountry use permit. Some cliffs

A climber jams a thin crack up Gem Wall, a vertical granite cliff at Lumpy Ridge.

are closed due to nesting raptors. Ask at a visitor center for information on closures, suggested climbs, and guidebooks. The Colorado Mountain School in Estes Park is the park's climbing concessionaire. They offer lessons and guided trips; see the Resources chapter.

Fishing

Although Rocky Mountain boasts 147 lakes, only 50 have fish populations. The rest of the lakes are too shallow and too cold to sustain viable populations through the harsh winters. Four species of trout—rainbow, brown, brook, and cutthroat—swim in the streams and lakes. The native species are the greenback cutthroat and the Colorado River cutthroat; with the greenback limited to catch-and-release. Many park waters are only catch-and-release with barbless hooks to maintain native trout. Lakes that allow keepers include Sprague Lake, Loch Vale, and Mills Lake. Some lakes are closed to fishing. All fishermen must have a Colorado fishing license. Only flies and lures are allowed, although children younger than age twelve may use bait some lakes. Ask at a visitor center for an updated list of closed waters.

Winter Sports

Rocky Mountain does not close in winter, but activities are curtailed by snow and cold. Nonetheless this is a great time to visit, since visitation is low. The lower elevation trails, like Gem Lake and Cub Lake trails, are usually passable. The best park areas for cross-country skiing and snowshoeing include Moraine Park, trails in the Bear Lake area, and Wild Basin. Equipment can be rented in Estes Park

k at a visitor center for info on snow nditions, suggested trips, and maps. owmobiling, while prohibited in the rk, is a popular pastime around Grand ke.

ducational Opportunities

e Rocky Mountain Nature Associa-
n has offered Rocky Mountain Field
minars since 1962. Most of these year-
und educational seminars, workshops,
d lectures begin at the Field Seminar
nter and continue out-of-doors in the
rk rather than in a classroom. Courses
nge from half day to several days and
n include programs in photography,
ture writing, Native American plant
ditions, fly fishing, GPS navigation,
imal behavior, forest and tundra ecol-
y, and local history. Some courses are
ered for children; others are available

for credit through Colorado State University. For information visit www.rmna.org or call (970) 586-3262.

Scenic Drives

Trail Ridge Road, the park's main scenic drive and the highest continuous paved highway (US 34) in the United States, connects Estes Park and Grand Lake by crossing lofty Trail Ridge. The road's high point is a lung-busting 12,187 feet above sea level. The 48-mile highway to the clouds, completed in 1932, follows a much older trail traveled by Native Americans as long ago as 12,000 years. The road offers stunning, expansive views from its 11-mile section above tree line and allows visitors to experience the park's alpine tundra. Allow at least four hours for driving, stops at overlooks, a short hike, and a visit to the Alpine Visitor Center.

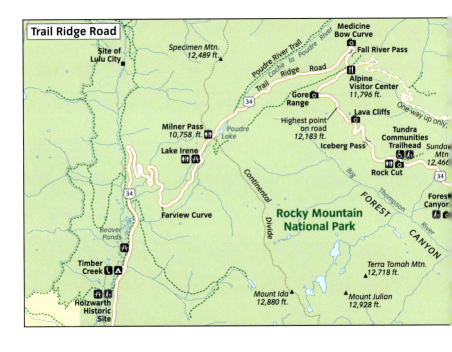

Trail Ridge Road

Site of Lulu City

Specimen Mtn. 12,489 ft.

Poudre River Trail

Cache la Poudre River

Medicine Bow Curve

Fall River Pass

Trail Ridge Road

Alpine Visitor Center 11,796 ft.

Gore Range

Highest point on road 12,183 ft.

Lava Cliffs

One-way up only;

Milner Pass 10,758 ft.

Poudre Lake

Lake Irene

Tundra Communities Trailhead

Sunda Mtn 12,466

Iceberg Pass

Rock Cut

Farview Curve

Continental Divide

Rocky Mountain National Park

FOREST

Big Thompson River

Forest Canyon

CANYON

Beaver Ponds

Timber Creek

Holzwarth Historic Site

Terra Tomah Mtn. 12,718 ft.

Mount Ida 12,880 ft.

Mount Julian 12,928 ft.

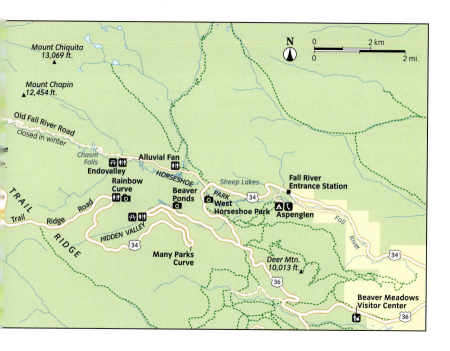

Mount Chiquita
13,069 ft.

Mount Chapin
12,454 ft.

Old Fall River Road
closed in winter

Chasm
Falls

Endovalley

Alluvial Fan

Rainbow
Curve

HORSESHOE

Beaver
Ponds

PARK

West
Horseshoe Park

Sheep Lakes

Fall River
Entrance Station

Aspenglen

TRAIL

Trail

Ridge

Road

RIDGE

HIDDEN VALLEY

34

Many Parks
Curve

Deer Mtn.
10,013 ft.

36

Fall

River

34

34

Beaver Meadows
Visitor Center

36

N

0   2 km

0   2 mi.

Summer Sensation

Take a July drive up Trail Ridge Road to its highest point to see a profusion of alpine wildflowers along the 0.5-mile Tundra Communities Trail.

Trail Ridge Road is usually open from Memorial Day to mid-October, depending on snowfall. Begin your trip to Rocky Mountain's rooftop at Deer Ridge Junction, 3 miles northwest of Beaver Meadows Visitor Center. Good viewpoints are found on the ascent: Many Parks Curve and Rainbow Curve, with great views into Horseshoe Park. Past Rainbow Curve the highway swings onto a steep mountainside and passes through a stunted

Visitors gaze into glacier-carved Forest Canyon from lofty Forest Canyon Overlook on Trail Ridge Road.

est of windswept trees at tree line. e next 11 miles are simply spectacular. p at Forest Canyon Overlook for views) a deep glacier-carved gorge; Rock : Overlook and Tundra Communities l, a 0.5-mile, out-and-back trail that)lores the fragile land above the trees; a Cliffs Overlook; Gore Range Over- k; and the Alpine Visitor Center with ibits and an adjoining snack bar and shop. Below the center the highway cends west to 10,758-foot Milner s on the Continental Divide and the idwaters of the Colorado River before tchbacking down to Kawuneeche ey.

l Fall River Road, for drivers who t more adventure, is a steep, wind- road that climbs 3,200 feet from seshoe Park to Fall River Pass and the ine Visitor Center atop Trail Ridge.

The one-way westbound road, with 9 miles of gravel, opened in 1920 after seven years of work and was the original east–west route through the park. It's open (summer only) for vehicles and mountain bikes, but vehicles longer than 25 feet and all trailers are prohibited. After driving the road, follow Trail Ridge Road back for a beautiful loop drive.

Bear Lake Road, beginning just west of the Beaver Meadows Entrance, runs 9 miles to Bear Lake, a lovely mountain

Parking tip: The Bear Lake Road parking lots fill quickly between 9:00 a.m. and 3:00 p.m. Instead of driving, take the free shuttle from the Park & Ride lot opposite Glacier Basin Campground.

Quaking Aspen

The leaves of the quaking aspen quiver and quake in the slightest breeze, giving it the proper name *Populus tremuloides,* from the Latin for "tremble." These tall, straight trees average 50 to 60 feet in height, live up to 120 years, and are usually found between 8,000 and 11,000 feet elevation in Rocky Mountain National Park. In September golden aspen leaves draw hordes of leaf-peepers to the hills just as the promise of gold ore once brought miners.

The lessened sunlight of autumn's short days coupled with cooling temperatures trigger the aspen's gaudy display. The production of chlorophyll—a green pigment leaves that manufactures carbohydrates by photosynthesis—slows and then stops. Other latent colors then emerge, including carotenoid compounds, the pigment that colors a carrot orange. A succession of bright September days stimulates these late colors to brilliantly adorn the aspen leaves under the waning rays of the summer sun. The color change begins in early September in the subalpine forest and then marches down the hillsides. Prime aspen viewing is during the last two weeks of the month. Great colors are found along Bear Lake Road, Fern and Cub Lake Trails, the lower slopes of Longs Peak, and Kawuneeche Valley.

Groves of quaking aspens bring colorful swaths of gold and orange to Rocky Mountain in late September.

lake nestled in the glacial valley below Hallett Peak. Along the way are the Moraine Park Museum, Sprague Lake, the trailhead for Glacier Gorge, and numerous hiking trails. The museum gives a great introduction to the park and its geology and natural history. Farther along are the Bierstadt Lake and Storm Pass Trailheads. Glacier Gorge Trailhead offers access to lovely Alberta Falls, the Loch, and Glacier Gorge. Bear Lake, lying at the road's end, is encircled by a paved half-mile path. You'll also find restrooms and a ranger station. Bear Lake Road is heavily traveled and congested in summer.

Just for Families

Rocky Mountain National Park is a kid-friendly place. Programs, walks, talks, and adventures cater to children and families. Here kids can be nature watchers by sitting and observing plants and animals, budding meteorologists by studying the sky and weather, or young adventurers by exploring creeks and trails.

Be a Junior Ranger

The park offers a popular Junior Ranger program for children ages five to twelve. About 15,000 children annually work toward their Junior Ranger badge by completing a logbook of self-guided activities and then reviewing the activities with a ranger. Some of the tasks include learning to keep the park clean and picking up trash;

The mostly flat Lily Lake Trail makes a perfect family adventure on a sunny summer afternoon.

not feeding wildlife; exploring the park's plants, animals, and birds; identifying ecosystems; and learning lightning safety and what to do if you're lost. After each child successfully completing the requirements, the ranger signs a certificate and awards the official Junior Ranger badge. Ask at any of the visitor centers to get your own Junior Ranger logbook.

Join in Ranger Adventures

Plenty of walks, talks, and campfire programs are suited for families. These are offered mostly from June through September. Pick up a current park newspaper for a list of offerings, dates, and times. A typical weekend Saturday in mid-July might include a tundra nature hike, a talk on Native Americans and the park, a Lily Lake wildflower hike, a kids' adventure hike at Sprague Lake, and a talk about "beaver basics"—all capped off with a campfire program at any of the park campgrounds or a ranger-led night hike. Ask at a visitor center for information on age-appropriate activities for your family.

The park visitor centers also make great family stops. At Fall River Visitor Center, kids can explore the Discovery Room, with its animal skins and large bronzes of park animals. The Moraine Park Museum, with exhibits designed by the Denver Museum of Nature and Science, offers hands-on displays of Rocky geology and glaciations.

Take a Hike

There's nothing like getting outside to explore the park, and Rocky Mountain, with its many trails, has lots of short,

sy hikes that are perfect for an after-
on family adventure. Bring along a
agnifying glass and binoculars to allow
ildren to discover the natural world.
s usually best to do short trails or
plore areas like lakeshores. Also keep
eye out for Rocky's famous wildlife.
re are some of the best hikes for
ungsters.

ar Lake Nature Trail. This easy, 0.6-
ile-long, paved path loops around Bear
ke, one of the park's most popular
kes. Come early or late to avoid the
owds. The *Bear Lake Nature Trail* pam-
let, available at the ranger station at
e lake, helps children understand the
ea's plants, wildlife, and geology.

oyote Valley Nature Trail. This mile-
ng educational trail makes a loop along
e Colorado River. This is a great hike

to see wildlife. Look for moose in the
willows, along with mule deer, elk, and
perhaps a wily coyote. The Arapahoe
Indians named this valley *Kawuneeche,*
meaning "Valley of the Coyote."

Gem Lake Trail. While this is a moder-
ately difficult trail, gaining over 1,000
feet from car to lake, it is a fun half-day
hike for kids. The trail ends at a small
lake tucked among granite cliffs. Along
the way kids can scramble on small
boulders or give fanciful names to rock
formations.

Moraine Park Interpretive Trail.
After visiting Moraine Park Museum, take
a hike on this easy 0.5-mile trail through
nearby meadows. Five interpretative
stops explore the park's geology, glaciers, weather, plants and animals, and
human impact.

Hey Ranger! Q & A Just for Kids

Q. What's the park's highest mountain?
A. Longs Peak is the highest mountain in the park at 14,259 feet above sea level. That's 2.7 miles high!

Q. When do the deer turn into elk?
A. Mule deer, the only deer found in the park, don't turn into elk. They're related to each other, along with moose, but they are separate species. You can tell the difference between elk and deer because elk are always bigger.

Q. Are there any snakes here?
A. The garter snake is the only snake and reptile found in the park. Look for these long, striped snakes at lower elevations near wetlands and creeks.

Q. Can we take the chipmunks home?
A. Nope. Rocky Mountain National Park is their home. You can't take anything—rocks, sticks, fossils, and animals—from the park. If everyone took something, what would be left?

Q. Do elk really have bugles?
A. Elk don't have bugles, but they do make a bugling noise. During the mating season in September and October, the male elk makes an eerie call that wildlife biologists call a bugle. It's hard to describe, but try to imagine deep notes that rise to a high squealing sound and then a bunch of loud grunts. Put those all together and you have an elk bugling!

What do ponderosa pines smell like?
It's a big debate as to what flavor
the pine smells like. Is it butterscotch?
Or is it vanilla? I'm in the butterscotch
camp myself. What do you think?

**What are those cute little guinea
pigs I see along Trail Ridge Road?**
Those are pikas, pronounced
"pie-ka." Pikas, related to rabbits, are
busy little mammals that spend all
summer cutting grass with sharp teeth
and then storing it in haypiles under
boulders so they have food to eat during winter. If you can't see them, you
can always hear their loud shrill whistle,
which often warns of predators.

Sprague Lake Nature Trail. This lovely
0.5-mile lakeside trail explores Sprague
Lake's shoreline. Expect great views;
benches for rests; wooden viewing
platforms over the water where kids can
sight trout, frogs, and beavers; and kid-
friendly fishing spots.

Tundra Communities Trail. One of
Rocky Mountain's best hikes, this 0.5-
mile paved trail crosses the fragile tundra
high above tree line. Kids enjoy colorful
wildflowers in summer, interpretative
displays, mushroom rocks, and a rocky
viewpoint at trail's end. Remember to
dress warmly and stay on the path to
avoid damaging plants.

Spot Wildlife

Rocky Mountain is like a big outdoor zoo.
Early morning and evening are the best

times to see lots of animals, especially big mammals. Bring binoculars to examine them up close and personal. Remember to follow wildlife-watching ethics by not stalking or bothering animals and not feeding them. Look for elk, mule deer, bighorn sheep, coyote, beaver, marmot, pika, Abert squirrel, chipmunks, and lots of bird species.

A budding Junior Ranger cools her heels in Sprague Lake, with its gorgeous views of the Continental Divide.

Recharge:
Places to sleep and eat

Most of Rocky Mountain is rugged and wild. Unlike many major national parks, Rocky doesn't have any lodging or many concessionaires within the park boundaries. Never fear—if your idea of "recharging" is spending the night outside under the starry night sky, you'll have plenty of choice "accommodations" in Rocky. Everything else you will want for food and shelter is just outside the park in the towns of Estes Park and Grand Lake (see the Beyond the Borders chapter).

Campsites

The park offers 587 campsites in five campgrounds as well as 267 backcountry sites that allow visitors to fully experience Rocky's serenity and beauty. Those who don't want to rough it can head out of the park to commercial campgrounds with amenities like hot showers and RV hookups.

On the east side of the park lie the two main campgrounds—Moraine Park and Glacier Basin Campgrounds, with 395 sites between them. Sites at both can be reserved from Memorial Day to September through National Park Reservation System (NPRS) at (877) 444-6777 or http://recreation.gov. Other camp-grounds on the east flank are Aspengle (54 sites) and Longs Peak (26 tent-only sites). Timber Creek Campground (98 sites) sits 7 miles north of the Grand La entrance. The latter three are first-com first-served. Get there early, especially summer, when they fill by midday. Grou sites are available at Moraine Park and Glacier Basin campgrounds.

Moraine Park, Longs Peak, and Tim-ber Creek are open year-round, but no

Park campground	Total sites	Dump stations	Reserve	Fees	Open
Aspenglen	54	No	No	$20	May–Sept.
Glacier Basin	150	Yes	Yes	$20	May–Sept.
Longs Peak	26	No	No	$14/$20	Year-round
Moraine Park	245	Yes	Yes	$14/$20	Year-round
Timber Creek	98	Yes	No	$14/$20	Year-round

ter is available in winter and spring. mp fees are $20 per night in summer th water; $14 in the off-season. There e no showers or RV hookups in any rk campgrounds. Pets are allowed but ust be always leashed. Camping is limd to seven days at all campgrounds. wer dump stations are at Moraine rk, Glacier Basin, and Timber Creek. ood fires are allowed in fire grates, but thering wood is prohibited. Firewood ndles are for sale at campgrounds and tside the park.

Private commercial campgrounds e found on both sides of the park for ers who crave more comforts than e park campgrounds offer. Near Estes rk are Elk Meadow Lodge & RV Park, es Park Campground, Estes Park KOA, ystone Park of Estes, Manor RV Park, ary's Lake Campground, National Park

Retreats, Paradise RV Park, and Spruce Lake RV Park. On the west at Grand Lake are Elk Creek Campground and Winding River Resort. All have full hookups, showers and bathhouses, laundries, stores, and activities.

Where to Eat

There are no full-service restaurants in the park. The only dining available in the park is at the snack bar in the Trail Ridge Store next to the Alpine Visitor Center atop Trail Ridge Road and at the Rocky Mountain Gateway Store next to the Fall River Visitor Center. Check out the Beyond the Borders chapter for suggestions for lodging and dining in Estes Park and Grand Lake.

Beyond the Borders:
Off-site places to sleep, eat, and go

Rocky Mountain National Park, split by the lofty Continental Divide, naturally divides into east and west sectors, with Estes Park and Grand Lake the respective gateway towns. Estes Park on the east, 70 miles from Denver, is the easiest accessed and busiest portal to the park. Grand Lake is quieter and smaller. Both provide all the services a visitor needs.

Estes Park

Estes Park nestles along the Big Thompson River in a high mountain valley at 7,522 feet. Above town stretches jaw-dropping scenery with wooded ridges, gray granite cliffs, and lofty glacier-gouged

Stunning autumn colors spread across mountainsides just outside the gateway towns of Estes Park and Grand Lake.

peaks. The bustling resort town is a pleasant, pedestrian-friendly place with more than 300 shops and restaurants and lots of lodging and entertainment choices.

Where to Stay

Estes Park and surrounding area offers lodging for every budget, including hotels, motels, bed-and-breakfast inns, RV parks, campgrounds, and guest ranches. Prices in the summer months are substantially higher than during the off-season, when bargains are found. For a complete listing go to the Estes Park Convention and Visitors Bureau Web site: www.estesparkcvb.com.

The Baldpate Inn, 4900 South Highway 7, P.O. Box 700, Estes Park 80517; (970) 586-6151; www.baldpateinn.com. The inn, 7 miles south of Estes Park

and across from Lily Lake, has housed folks in its main lodge and cabins since 1917. Listed on the National Register of Historic Places, the Baldpate offers great views and the world's largest key collection with 30,000 keys. Its award-winning restaurant serves only homemade soups, salads, bread, and pies.

Black Canyon Inn, 800 MacGregor Avenue, Estes Park 80517; (800) 897-3730, (970) 586-8113; www.blackcanyoninn .com. Nestled on fourteen wooded acres near downtown Estes Park, the inn offers suites and a rustic cabin with mountain views, fireplaces, kitchens, and a heated outdoor pool. Eat at Twin Owls Steakhouse Restaurant housed in a 1929 log building.

Marys Lake Lodge, 2625 Marys Lake Road, Estes Park 80517; (877) 442-6279, (970) 586-5958; www.maryslakelodge

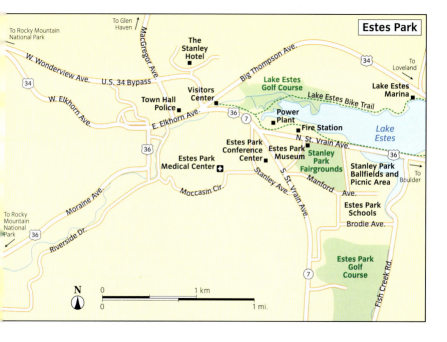

Estes Park

To Glen Haven

To Rocky Mountain National Park

W. Wonderview Ave.

MacGregor Ave.

U.S. 34 Bypass

Big Thompson Ave.

To Loveland

34

34

The Stanley Hotel

W. Elkhorn Ave.

Town Hall Police

Visitors Center

Lake Estes Golf Course

Lake Estes Bike Trail

Lake Estes Marina

36

7

Power Plant

Fire Station

Lake Estes

E. Elkhorn Ave.

N. St. Vrain Ave.

36

Estes Park Conference Center

Estes Park Museum

Stanley Park Fairgrounds

Stanley Park Ballfields and Picnic Area

To Boulder

Estes Park Medical Center

Moccaisn Cir.

Stanley Ave.

S. St. Vrain Ave.

Manford Ave.

Moraine Ave.

Estes Park Schools

Brodie Ave.

To Rocky Mountain Park

36

Riverside Dr.

7

Estes Park Golf Course

Fish Creek Rd.

N

0   1 km

0   1 mi.

.com. This chalet lodge, open since 1913, overlooks Mary's Lake south of Estes Park. The hotel offers sixteen rooms in the main lodge, two restaurants, and a spa. Original woodwork, antiques, and claw-foot bathtubs are found in some rooms.

Romantic RiverSong Bed & Breakfast Inn, 1766 Lower Broadview Road, Estes Park 80517; (970) 586-4666; www .romanticriversong.com. Voted Colorado's Best Romantic Getaway, this secluded B&B lies on twenty-seven wooded acres threaded with trails and serenaded by birdsong. The inn offers ten guest rooms and several cottages, a choice of thirty different breakfasts, and five-course dinners on bone china.

The Stanley Hotel, 333 East Wonderview Avenue, Estes Park 80517; (800) 976-1377, (970) 586-3371; www .stanleyhotel.com. The Stanley, one of Colorado's grand old hotels and a National Historic Landmark, sits on a hill with a commanding view of Estes Park. Opened in 1909, it was the world first hotel with electricity and in-room telephones. The five-story Georgian-style hotel inspired Stephen King's nov *The Shining.* Its 157 rooms offer scenic views, modern conveniences, and antiques.

Swiftcurrent Lodge, 2512 Highway 6 Estes Park 80517; (888) 639-9673, (970 586-3720; www.swiftcurrentlodge.cor Swiftcurrent Lodge is located 300 yarc from Rocky Mountain National Park an 3 miles southwest of downtown Estes Park. Hiking trails begin right at your door. Enjoy fishing the Big Thompson River only steps from your door.

YMCA of the Rockies—Estes Park Center, 2515 Tunnel Road, Estes Park

511; (800) 777-9622; www.ymca ck ies.org. This 890-acre property cludes 688 rooms in lodges and 220 bins. The family-friendly center has a sbee golf course, climbing wall, res-urant, tennis court, pool, and gym.

here to Eat

tes Park is flush with dining establish-ents that range from basic come-as-ou-are eateries to ritzy restaurants. The llowing are a few recommendations.

ig Horn Restaurant, 401 West Elk-orn, Estes Park 80517; (970) 586-2792; ww.estesparkbighorn.com. The Big orn offers casual dining and great reakfasts with pancakes, waffles, break-st burritos, and giant omelets. The nch and dinner menu has steaks, Mexi-an food, pasta, and BBQ. Open seven ays a week at 6:00 a.m. $4 to $17.

Cascades Restaurant, 333 Wonderview Avenue, Estes Park 80517; (800) 976-1377, (970) 586-3371; www.stanleyhotel. com. Dine on the patio, outside beside a waterfall, or indoors by a fire and enjoy classy American cuisine in the restau-rant of the elegant Stanley Hotel. The menu features regional dishes, including Colorado game, and a large wine list. Open for breakfast, lunch, and dinner seven days a week. Reservations recom-mended. $10 to $40.

Dunraven Inn, 2470 Highway 66, Estes Park 80517; (970) 586-6409; www .dunraveninn.com. This romantic res-taurant, named for the Earl of Dunraven, the original baron of Estes Park, has served diners since 1931. Try the fresh fish, prime steaks, or Italian specialties. Reservations recommended. $10 to $40.

Poppy's Pizza & Grill, 342 East Elkhorn Avenue, Estes Park 80517; (970) 586-8282; www.poppyspizzaandgrill.com. Create your own superb mountain pizza from five sauces and forty-plus toppings or try one of the excellent specialty pies—like one with smoked trout, capers, and cream cheese; or the Mexican, hummus, or Thai pizzas. Also burgers and daily specials. $8 to $22. Closed January.

Sweet Basilico Café, 430 Prospect Drive, Estes Park 80517; (970) 586-3899; www.sweetbasilico.com. This small Italian eatery dishes up favorites like minestrone soup, stuffed manicotti, lasagna, and eggplant Parmesan as well as tasty sandwiches. Reservations recommended. $7 to $20.

What to Do

Estes Park offers a wealth of activities.

Practice rock climbing skills on an artificial wall, learn how to fly cast, visit local historic sites, boat around Lake Estes, play a scenic round of golf, ride an aerial tram up Prospect Mountain, or T-shirt shop 'til you drop. The town hosts festivals in the warmer months and musical entertainment around town, including a Performance Park Amphitheater. Check with the Estes Park Convention and Visitors Bureau (www.estesparkcvb.com) for a complete listing of activities. Here are some favorites to get you started.

Aerial Tramway, 420 East Riverside Drive, Estes Park 80517; (970) 586-3675; www.estestram.com. Let the tram, built in 1955, whisk you to the top of Prospect Mountain, a lofty 1,400 feet above Estes Park, for excellent views of the town and surrounding mountains. Open mid-May to mid-September. $9 for adults, $8 over

eat hiking trails and climbing cliffs at Lily Lake e south of Estes Park.

ge sixty, $4 ages six to eleven, free nder age five.

nos Mills Cabin, 6760 Colorado Highay 7, Estes Park 80517; (970) 586-4706; ttp://home.earthlink.net/~enosmillscbn. ocated 8 miles south of Estes Park, his site explores the life and writings of nos Mills, the father of Rocky Moun-

tain National Park. Visit Mills's original log cabin, built in 1885, and peruse a wonderful collection of his nature photographs. Open Wednesday, Thursday, and Friday 10:00 a.m. to 3:00 p.m. from June through September; by reservation the rest of the year. $5.00 for adults, $2.50 children ages 6 to 12.

The Estes Park Museum, 200 Fourth Street, Estes Park 80517; (970) 586-6256; www.estesnet.com/museum. Founded in 1962, this museum preserves and interprets local history from the Utes to early settlers to the national park. Check out memorabilia and historical artifacts like one of the original Stanley Steamers built by F. O. Stanley. Temporary exhibits on area art and history appear through the year. Open daily May through September and Friday to Sunday from January through April. Free.

The Historic Fall River Hydroplant, 1754 Fish Hatchery Road, Estes Park 80517; (970) 586-6256; www.estesnet.com/hydroplant. Built by F. O. Stanley to power the Stanley Hotel, the plant was damaged in the Lawn Lake Flood and ceased operation in 1982. Its restoration as a museum won several awards. The site is listed on the National Register of Historic Places. Open Tuesday through Sunday 1:00 to 4:00 p.m. from the day after Memorial Day to the day before Labor Day. Free.

MacGregor Ranch and Museum, 180 MacGregor Avenue, Estes Park 80517; (970) 586-3749; www.macgregorranch.org. Learn about homesteading and cattle ranching at this 1,200-acre, 1870s working ranch in the valley below Lumpy Ridge. Be sure to visit the 1873 MacGregor family home, which doubles as a museum. Open Tuesday through Friday from June through August. Free.

Grand Lake

The village of Grand Lake, founded in 1881, offers a look into old Colorado with its old buildings and rustic look—it not all condos yet! Lying on the north shore of Colorado's largest natural lake at 8,369 feet, the town is just east of US 34 after it exits Rocky's western entrance. The quaint town is surrounde by mountains and forests and makes a great base camp for exploring the park' western reaches. The lake offers good fishing for trout and salmon and is home to the world's highest yacht club. The area is called the Snowmobiling Capital of Colorado for its deep snows and mile of trails in Arapaho National Forest.

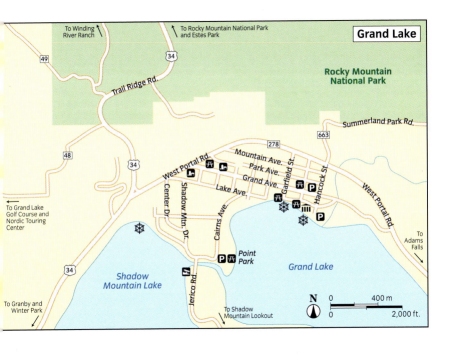

Grand Lake

To Winding River Ranch

To Rocky Mountain National Park and Estes Park

49

34

Rocky Mountain National Park

Trail Ridge Rd.

Summerland Park Rd.

663

48

34

278

Mountain Ave.

West Portal Rd.

Park Ave.

Grand Ave.

Garfield St.

Hancock St.

West Portal Rd.

To Grand Lake Golf Course and Nordic Touring Center

Center Dr.

Shadow Mtn. Dr.

Lake Ave.

Cairns Ave.

Jerico Rd.

P

Point Park

Shadow Mountain Lake

34

To Granby and Winter Park

To Shadow Mountain Lookout

Grand Lake

P

To Adams Falls

N

0   400 m

0   2,000 ft.

Where to Stay

Accommodations include hotels, motels, bed-and-breakfast inns, dude ranches, campgrounds, and rental cabins. The Grand Lake Chamber of Commerce (www.grandlakechamber.com) has complete listings and contact information. The following are a few suggestions.

Bighorn Lodge, 613 Grand Avenue, Grand Lake 80447; (888) 315-2378, (970) 627-8101; www.bighornlodge.net. The twenty-seven-room lodge is close to the national park's west entrance and convenient for shopping, fishing, and winter sports.

C Lazy U Ranch, 3640 Colorado Highway 125, P.O. Box 379, Granby 80446; (970) 887-3344; www.clazyu.com. This ultimate deluxe dude ranch boasts a real Colorado ranch heritage. Spread across a high valley, C Lazy U offers forty beautiful accommodations and twenty guest cabins, superb meals, lots of outdoor adventures, and your own horse. There are plenty of kids' programs. The minimum stay is three days, with a Wednesday or Saturday arrival in summer, and two nights in winter.

The Historic Rapids Lodge & Restaurant, 209 Rapids Lane, Grand Lake 80447; (970) 627-3707; www.rapids lodge.com. The lodge, built in 1915, and its excellent restaurant sit alongside Tonahutu River. The seven lodge rooms are decorated with antiques and claw-foot tubs. Eleven modern condos and five rustic cabins are options. Close April and November.

Western Riviera Motel & Cabins, 419 Garfield, Grand Lake 80447; (970) 627-

80; www.westernriv.com. Lakeside
dging at its best—sixteen lakeside
otel rooms, ten lakeside cabins, one
keside two-bedroom condo, and twelve
ourtyard cabins near the west entrance
Rocky Mountain National Park. Open
ear-round. Long-term winter rentals.

here to Eat

rand Lake and nearby Granby and Win-
r Park offer the only dining establish-
ents on the west side of the national
ark.

he Grand Lake Brewing Company,
15 Grand Avenue, Grand Lake 80447;
970) 627-1711; www.grandlakebrewing
om. This brew pub offers a diverse
election of brewed beers, including
laid Bastard and White Cap Wheat,
oth gold medal winners at the Colorado
State Fair. It also serves pub food such
as sandwiches and appetizers and sells
beer to go. $5 to $8.

Rapids Restaurant, 209 Rapids Lane,
Grand Lake 80447; (970) 627-3707; www
.rapidslodge.com. Come for excellent
fine dining in the rustic Rapids Restaurant overlooking the Tonahutu River. The
unique regional cuisine includes entrees
like elk medallions, trout, and stuffed
portobello mushrooms. Extensive wine
list. Open daily in summer at 5:00 p.m.
and Wednesday through Sunday in winter. Closed April and November. Reservations recommended. $22 to $38.

Sagebrush BBQ and Grill, 1101 Grand
Avenue, Grand Lake 80447; (970) 627-
1404; http://sagebrushbbq.com. Tasty
American cuisine in a pleasant cafe that
is like an old-time western roadhouse

with peanut shells chucked on the floor. Try the ribs, chicken, and catfish with sides of comfort food or order the elk or buffalo burgers. They also serve vegetarian meals and breakfasts. $4 to $23.

What to Do

Grand Lake, settled in 1876 as a mining supply center, offers year-round outdoor activities. Summer is ideal for lake fun. Take a walk along the boardwalk on a summer's evening, cast a fishing line into the lake or a nearby river, or rent a boat for a jaunt around the lake. In winter go cross-country skiing or snowmobiling. Farther south is Winter Park, one of Colorado's major ski resorts.

Grand Lake Golf Course, 1415 CR 48, Grand Lake 80447; (800) 551-8580, (970) 627-8008; www.grandlakegolf.com. This eighteen-hole championship golf course lying at 8,420 feet, offers challenging shots and spectacular views of the Never Summer Range. Keep an eye out from the tee for passing elk, deer, and moose.

Grand Lake Touring Center, 1415 CR 48, Grand Lake 80447; (970) 627-8008; www.grandlakegolf.com/touring. The center offers 35 kilometers of groomed cross-country skiing trails from beginner to advanced as well as scenic views of the national park. Ski rentals and lessons are available.

Resources

Rocky Mountain National Park,
1000 Highway 36, Estes Park, CO 80517-8397; www.nps.gov/romo
Visitor information: (970) 586-1206
Visitor information recorded message: (970) 586-1333
Visitor information for the hearing impaired (TTY): (970) 586-1319
Backcountry Office: (970) 586-1242
Campground reservations: (877) 444-6777

Rocky Mountain Nature Association,
48 Alpine Circle, P.O. Box 3100, Estes Park, CO 80517; (970) 586-0108; www.rmna.org

Rocky Mountain Nature Association Field Seminars, 1895 Fall River Road,

Estes Park, CO 80517; (970) 586-3262; fieldseminars@rmna.org

Estes Park Convention and Visitors Bureau, Estes Park Visitors Center, 500 Big Thompson Avenue, P.O. Box 1200, Estes Park, CO 80517; (800) 44-ESTES, (970) 577-9900; http://estesparkcvb.com

Grand Lake Chamber of Commerce,
P.O. Box 429, Grand Lake, CO 80447; (800) 531-1019, (970) 627-3402; www.grandlakechamber.com

Grand County Colorado Tourism Board, P.O. Box 131, Granby, CO 80446; (800) 247-2636; www.grand-county.com

Climbing Guides and Stores

Colorado Mountain School, 2829 Mapleton Avenue, Boulder, CO 80301; (800) 836-4008, (303) 447-2804; www .totalclimbing.com

Estes Park Mountain Shop, 2050 Big Thompson Avenue, Estes Park, CO 80517; (866) 303-6548, (970) 586-6548; http://estesparkmountainshop.com

Flyfishing Supplies and Guides

Alpine Flyfishing Outfitters, 140 East Elkhorn, P.O. Box 1511, Estes Park, CO 80517; (970) 577-9231; www.alpinefly fishingoutfitters.com

Estes Adventures, P.O. Box 792, Estes Park, CO 80517; (970) 577-0226, (970) 231-0887; www.estesadventures.com

Estes Angler, 338 West Riverside Drive P.O. Box 1703, Estes Park, CO 80517; (800) 586-2110, (970) 586-2110; www .estesangler.com

Kirks Flyshop, 230 East Elkhorn Avenue, Estes Park, CO 80517; (970) 577-0790; www.kirksflyshop.com

Rocky Mountain Adventures, 1117 North Highway 287, Fort Collins, CO 80524; (800) 858-6808, (970) 493-4005; www.shoprma.com

Scot's Sporting Goods, 870 Moraine Avenue, Estes Park CO 80517; (970) 586 2877; http://scotssportinggoods.com.

Hiking Guides

Estes Adventures, P.O. Box 792, Estes Park, CO 80517; (970) 577-0226, (970) 231-0887; www.estesadventures.com

Kaiyote Tours/Kaiyote Snow, P.O. Box 301, Estes Park, CO 80517; (970) 556-103; www.kaiyotetours.com

Horseback Riding

Aspen Lodge, 6120 Highway 7, Estes Park, CO 80517; (970) 586-8133; www.aspenlodge.net

Hi Country Stables, 1000 Bear Lake Road, Estes Park, CO 80517; (970) 586-3244 (in park in summer): Moraine Park (970) 586-2327; Glacier Creek (970) 586-3244; www.colorado-horses.com/hicountrystables

Meeker Park Lodge, 11733 Highway 7, Allenspark, CO 80510; (303) 747-2266

Silver Lane Stables, P.O. Box 152, Estes Park, CO 80517; (970) 586-4695; www.silverlanestables.com

S.K. Horses, P.O. Box 2214, Estes Park, CO 80517; Cowpoke Corner Corral (970) 586-9272; National Park Gateway Stables (970) 586-5269; www.cowpokecornercorral.com

Sombrero Ranch, Inc., 3300 Airport Road, Boulder, CO 80301; Estes Park Stable (970) 586-4577; Grand Lake Stable (970) 627-3514; Allenspark Stable (303) 747-2551; Glen Haven Stable (970) 586-2669; www.sombrero.com

Wild Basin Livery, P.O. Box 218, Allenspark, CO 80510; (303) 747-2274; www.wildbasinlodge.com

Winding River Resort, P.O. Box 629, Grand Lake, CO 80447; (970) 627-3215; www.windingriverresort.com

YMCA of the Rockies, 2515 Tunnel Road, Estes Park, CO 80511; (970) 586-3341; http://jacksonstables.com

Index

FALCONGUIDES®

Copyright © 2008 Morris Book Publishing, LLC

Falcon and FalconGuides are registered trademarks of Morris Book Publishing, LLC.
Popout is a trademark of Compass Maps, Ltd.
popout™ map and associated products are the subject of patents pending worldwide.

Photos by Stewart M. Green
Text design by Mary Ballachino
Maps created by XNR Productions, Inc. © Morris Book Publishing, LLC

Library of Congress Cataloging–in–Publication Data is available.
ISBN 978-0-7627-4808-2

Printed in China
10 9 8 7 6 5 4 3 2 1